NUDE MODELLING
FOR THE AFTERLIFE

NUDE MODELLING FOR THE AFTERLIFE

HENRY NORMAL

BLOODAXE BOOKS

ISBN: 1 85224 279 5

First published 1993 by
Bloodaxe Books Ltd,
P.O. Box 1SN,
Newcastle upon Tyne NE99 1SN.

Bloodaxe Books Ltd acknowledges
the financial assistance of Northern Arts.

Cover printing by J. Thomson Colour Printers Ltd, Glasgow.

Printed in Great Britain by
Bell & Bain Limited, Glasgow, Scotland.

to my dad
FRANCIS JAMES CARROLL

Acknowledgements

Some of these poems were published in Henry Normal's previous small press collections: *Do You Believe in Carpetworld?* (Purple Heather, 1988); *Is Love Science Fiction?* (1986), *Love Like Hell* (1988), *Does Inflation Affect the Emotions?* (1989), *A More Intimate Fame* (1990) and *The Dream Ticket* (1991), published by A Twist in the Tale; and *Fifteenth of February* (1992) and *The Third Person* (1993) from Sheffield Popular Publishing.

Acknowledgements are also due to the editors of the following publications in which some of these poems first appeared: *City Life*, *High on the Walls: A Morden Tower Anthology* (Morden Tower/ Bloodaxe, 1990), *The Popular Front of Contemporary Poetry* (Apples & Snakes, 1992) and *Slow Dancer*.

Some of the poems have been read on the following television and radio stations and programmes: Channel Four (*Packet of Three*), Granada Television (*The New*), Border Television (*Word of Mouth*), BBC Radio 4 (*Kaleidoscope*), BBC Radio 5, BBC Radio Sheffield, GMR, Piccadilly Radio, BBC Radio Nottingham, Radio Trent, BBC Radio Derby and BBC Radio Merseyside.

Contents

Love like Hell

I have this theory that when you die your whole life is re-run like a sensorama video and you have to sit through it all again, every second, unedited, in a room with every friend and every relative that's been in the least bit involved. Now depending on what sort of life you've led this could be Heaven or it could be Hell. Think about it, everyone's going to see those private moments, those very private moments: farting in the bath; wiping bogies down the side of the armchair; every second of indulgent masturbation.

All the pathetic lies you told exposed for all to see; all the naff chat-up lines you used when you were a teenager, and still used later; all the places you had sex when you still lived at home. The things you did to get by; the way you justified it all to yourself and every really dumb-arsed no-balls shit-for-brains mistake you ever made you'll have to watch yourself make again. But then
      maybe
             there'll be those moments of rare beauty; the moments of tenderness; the times you cried because you messed up; the things you meant to say; the questions in the mirror; the promises you made when you first held your own child; the nights you comforted another's despair; the time your lover's face glowed like beauty on fire; the times you said 'I love you' and believed your love would outlive the universe. The time you first held in your stomach thinking no one would notice, and the regret in your eyes when you feared you were getting old. When you couldn't sleep one night and lay awake sweating and praying you didn't die before doing something, something, just something.

It's only a theory, and in my more optimistic moods I like to think that maybe there'll be a pause and a rewind for the good moments, and a fast forward for the rest.

The poem with no name

In the movie
he rode away into the sunset.
But the next day
I saw him shopping
in Tesco. Some check-out
woman gave him a bad time
and he never even shot
her once. Which only
goes to prove Tesco
isn't like real life at all.

Fallacy of the lower middle class

And on the 8th day, God created the lower middle class and he spoke saying take from these terraced slums my working-class people that they may settle in the new promised land we shall call council estates and give unto them extended credit facilities with no deposit and whole manner of consumer goods. Let them purchase venetian blinds, electric door bells which play ten much loved tunes and go forth to Spain for their holiday of a lifetime bringing back a 3ft donkey and some genuine reproduction maracas.

Let them install fitted carpets, central heating and Japanese hi-fi systems into their abode. Surround them with images of style and culture that they may dwell in their illusion.

And unto them furnish sons and daughters that they may grow strong in their pretensions and flee from these places called council estates saying – 'Get thee behind me social stigma'.

And let these sons and daughters visit tasteful restaurants for evening meals and let them buy basket work and matching pine from arty shops that charge outrageous prices. And let these sons and daughters read the *Daily Mail* and go out in foursomes to the local lounge and talk about loft insulation, patio doors and stone fireplaces. And never, never, call these people working-class for these are to be termed the lower middle class for verily the term working-class is to be cast out from this land for ever and ever. Amen.

There is love at first sight

There is wonder in attraction
the dancing of light on the retina
the alignment of atoms into form and substance
the perception of science as nature

Anatomy and biology raised to aesthetics and beauty
the tautness of flesh over muscle and frame
the way fabric clings to an outline
the contours of a rib cage
the tilt of a pelvis
the enticement of hollows and shadows
poise and the grace of texture

Colours and tones that blend and sculpt the imagination
the vulnerability of a neckline
the fragrance of moisture and the lure of intoxication
the glow of touch and the genius of the blood's energy
there is miracle in personality
there is wonder in attraction
there is love at first sight
I am already yours

Welcome to the City of Self

*(the above phrase was found graffitied on the art gallery
at Edinburgh during the Fringe 1990)*

Welcome to the City of Self
Where the body of Christ becomes bread and jam
The beast with a thousand I's
I leaflet therefore I am

Winning boat races tie at Oxbridge
Careerists frigging in the ligging
It's the death of a sales pitch
Where the one-line quote is King

Where it takes 200 to tango
Fast talking at the running buffet
Is there a medical student in the house?
Or is everyone's name really 'lovey'?

Beauty hangs its head
Where the commonplace has no worth
Where once the touch of another hand
Might have been the greatest show on Earth

There's an old man dead in the gutter
There are razor blades stained by a bath
But in the carnival nothing else matters
Except he who gets the last laugh

Tuning up with the 'me me me'
The sell by date of the year
If Van Gogh had had to play Edinburgh
He'd have cut off his other ear

A tender moment

I love you…no I mean I *really* love you.

Do you love me? Really?

Only I'm always telling you I love you but you
never say you love me only when I say it first
and then you say 'I love you too' but never first.

You know it'd be nice if you said it first.
Said 'I love you' without me having to say
I love you first.

No it doesn't count now.

I sometimes wonder if you really love me, you know,
really.
I mean what do you love about me?

There must be something.

Don't just say you don't know.

I don't know, it doesn't count if I say it.

Oh forget it, you're bloody useless.

The dream ticket

…Man with obvious disability in maintaining relationships seeks all consuming passion but will settle for friendship and the occasional shag. Doesn't believe relationships ever work but has been known to fake undue optimism.

Woman must be classic beauty, half saint half whore (ONO). Must be 100 per cent loyal but tolerant of bumbling indiscretion. Must have no friends that she wouldn't ditch just to spend a few extra seconds in my presence. Romantic but practical. Have good sense of humour but still laugh at my weak puns.

Must be available to lavish attention on me whenever I need pampering but have interesting things to do when I'm busy so that I can be entertained when we next meet.

Must have no friends that are male, unless they are grossly ugly. All female friends should be incredibly horny and desperate to sleep with me given the slightest chance.

Must be caring and gentle in bed but willing to be ravished, tied up and have various substances smeared over specified portions of the anatomy. Must come very loudly every time we have sex. Must synchronise with each of my orgasms. Must groan and moan softly until the final stages then shout such comments as 'I've never had it so good', 'You're so big' and 'God, I love you'.

Must burst into tears for no reason occasionally and when challenged say, 'I don't want to lose you'.

Must hate every one of my male friends. Find them sexually repulsive and inferior to me in every way. Must understand that my female friends are just friends and that's different.

Must always have a worse time than me at parties. Must hate parties, students, arty wankers, wanky art students, parties with wanky art students.

Must be completely naive innocent and optimistic but worldwise. Must be young at heart but sensible. Must be practically a virgin but have a sophisticated knowledge of sexual technique.

Must be intelligent but not so it makes me realise my simplistic thought processes.

Most importantly must realise that all the above is not a joke.

Send tasteful nude photo, to some anonymous box number.

Prayers for the imperfect

We are the imperfect
the rejected
the bruised
the damaged goods
the mishapen fruit

the crop that failed to make the grade
the eggshell that couldn't take the strain
the discounted
the allowable waste
the below standard
the bottom of the range
the potatoes with too many eyes
the slow mover putrified
the garment soiled
the bargain spoiled
the chipped and cracked
the squeezed and put back
the peas no longer tender and young
the incomplete
the thread undone
the scorned
the squashed
the marked down
the grape unwashed

We are the imperfect
the rejected
the bruised
the aborted
the discontinued

Let's pretend

Let's pretend we're both drunk and you're not married
and I'm not courting that girl in the kitchen and nobody
can see us and we don't know what we're doing and you put
your hand down my trousers whilst I lick your nipples and
if anyone comes in and finds us we were only pretending.

And because it's dark we can pretend to fumble about and
grope at each other's crotch and buttocks and you can drape
your knickers over my head whilst I bend you over the chair
and if people should say anything we can pretend it was only
innocent party games and when we sink to the ash-stained
carpet exhausted and unkempt we can pretend it was great and
even that we share something special and then you can go back
to your husband and I to my girlfriend and pretend.

The ugly duckling that grew up to be an ugly duck

At teenage discos both the male and the female of the species would travel in pairs.

These would generally be termed the Goodlooking one and the Uglybastard.

A standard ploy of the Goodlooking one to create cohesion would be to say,
'It's so difficult to find a partner because there's usually a Goodlooking one and an Uglybastard, and we're both goodlooking'.

This the Uglybastard would tend to believe.
Being both ugly and stupid
and because, of course,
deep down they wanted to believe it, whether true or not.

In fact sometimes the Uglybastard would actually think that they were indeed the Goodlooking one and feel sorry for the other poor schmuck not realising that the only reason the Goodlooking one was palling about with them in the first place was that they were no competition.

At this point the Uglybastard would say,
'It's so difficult to find a partner because there's usually a Goodlooking one and an Uglybastard, and we're both goodlooking'.

The only exception to this rule is when both are Uglybastards. (Although to create a bond the exact same wording would again be used)

Love turned green

She inflicted her love like a wound
and only with her hand laid on the wound
and only when it wept did she have faith in her love
it was a love that cowered in doorways
a love that talked in accusations
where the words 'I love you' became a threat
and where love hung like terror over every chance remark.

The house is not the same since you left

The house is not the same since you left
the cooker is angry – it blames me
The TV tries desperately to stay busy
but occasionally I catch it staring out of the window
The washing-up's feeling sorry for itself again
it just sits there saying 'What's the point, what's the
point?'
The curtains count the days
Nothing in the house will talk to me
I think your armchair's dead
The kettle tried to comfort me at first
but you know what its attention span's like
I've not told the plants yet
they still think you're on holiday
The bathroom misses you
I hardly see it these days
It still can't believe you didn't take it with you
The bedroom won't even look at me
since you left it keeps it's eyes closed
all it wants to do is sleep, remembering better times
trying to lose itself in dreams
it seems like it's taken the easy way out
but at night I hear the pillows
weeping into the sheets.

Love poem to the reviewers

I wish upon you a pox
Spuds in your favourite sox
I hope you die
With the LP of your life
Marked down in the cheapie box

May you rot and burn in Hell
May you choke on your own pissy smell
May the fluff in your navel
Drive you unstable
And may you suffer from verrucas as well

May all your conkers be oners
May you love life fail with dishonours
May your victories be small
And your enemies be tall
All driving thirty-two tonners

May your bath water always run cold
May your road maps never refold
May you lose all your diaries
And may Directory Enquiries
Keep you on permanent hold

The last poem I ever wrote

The last poem I ever wrote I had such high hopes for.

The last poem I ever wrote was to have been so powerful it would make war obsolete and nuclear fusion as vital as trainspotting. It was to have been so cleverly constructed it would hold the key to the very universe itself, make Arthur C. Clarke redundant and James Burke intelligible; so full of life it would be strapped onto wounds, and made into tablets and ointment. The Olympic committee would disqualify competitors found to have read it. Laid over the face of a child's corpse it would bring the dead back to life.

The last poem I ever wrote was published in a low budget poetry magazine boasting a print run of 220, 150 of which still remain under the editor's bed. The title escapes me but it was some pathetic pun such as *Write Now*.

The last poem I ever wrote was performed to an alternative cabaret audience at Cleethorpes off-season in between an alternative juggler and a 22-piece Catalonian dance band. Coinciding with the call for last orders it was heckled constantly by a drunk born and bred in London who sang in a Scotch accent and claimed to own the city of Glasgow personally.

The last poem I ever wrote was entered in a poetry competition by a lifelong enemy. The judges having been certified dead were suitably appointed as their names were unknown even to each other let alone to anyone else. My poem came 63rd out of seven million entries and won a year's subscription to the Crumpsall Poetry Appreciation Society Crochet Circle and Glee Club Gazette.

The last poem I ever wrote was cremated along with my body, unread.

The last poem I ever wrote was carried in the hearts of those I loved.

Never play chess with an Anarcho-Nihilist

I tried to play chess with an Anarcho-Nihilist once.
Every move I made – he questioned.

He continually changed the rules
But later claimed that there weren't really any in the first place.

He said 'Any piece can go to any position on the board it wants,
when it wants'.

He kept making three or four moves at a time. Then, when it
suited him, he moved my pieces out of the way. Sometimes into
other rooms.

He refused to place any of the pieces centrally in the proper
squares. He declared such divisions to be 'False Borders' and
started painting out the white squares at random.

When I announced it was check mate and that I'd won
He just kicked the table over and
Flushed my King down the loo.

Puppy love – a dog's life

Whatever happened to little Julie Bowers? She was classy.

I'd never seen anyone so clean, she must have washed every day. Proper leather school satchel with the straps and buckles and everything, just like in the *Bunty* comics. Not that I read *Bunty* comics, sometimes I cut out the outfits on the back cover.

Luckily around this time I discovered masturbation, so I no longer had to hang from playground equipment to achieve that pleasant tingling sensation in my groin.

But Julie Bowers was above all that, she was classy.

She was the kind of girl who would never fool around behind the library curtains. I was just a scruffy kid with snotty sleeves and hand-me-downs from an older sister, our love could never be. She lived in the posh part of the council estate where the houses had hedges too thick to dive through. She was unattainable, a Goddess.

She had the complete set of felt-tip colours, the full range with light and dark brown. To her jigsaws were fun. She entered all the Blue Peter competitions and she could read *Look And Learn* without faking it. She was classy alright, something of a playground intellectual and I respected her mind, though in my weaker moments I just wanted her to snog me to a state of total exhaustion. That seductive overbite, the cute turned-up nose, her neat ponytail, pleated skirt and those knee length white socks, she knew how to drive a boy wild.

Yes she was classy, mind you round our way any girl who ate with her mouth closed was considered classy.

What could I do? I tried to drown my sorrows in Taunton's cider but developed chronic flatulence instead. Were these really to be the happiest days of my life?

Prehistoric courtship

Menfolk tell of a fabled creature
called the female orgasm
it comes in the night
and it's so enormous
it makes your hair stand on end and your toes curl.
Menfolk enact a strange dance
to conjure up the spirit of the mythical beast
but this usually brings forth only the male of the species
which is smaller and thought to resemble a slug
due to its sticky trail.
It is said the beast could be brought forth
if the menfolk didn't engage in the preliminary
12 pints of lager ritual

...but that's old wives' tales.

Love by list

You're new to my list of acquaintances
let us list the things we have in common.
I like your lists – here is a list of good points I've spotted
here is a list of things for us to say, and a list of other lists that
will come in handy.

I love you, see under list no.14
for response.
You are not responding correctly
have you read your lists? Here is a
list of things you are doing wrong.
Here is another list, you will see some
items have been duplicated.

I'm afraid I've lost the list with
your good points, but it's OK
I'm too busy keeping all these
lists together.

I'm going to have to
take you off my list of active
relationships, still don't worry
I have a list for you
we can put you here under failures.

Sans pretension

We say 'cul de sac'
To make 'dead end' sound sunny.
We say 'nouveau riche'
Instead of – working class with money.

We call art 'avant-garde'
When we don't understand it.
Jumble sales sell 'bric-à-brac'
Which must be French for shit.

Let's call a spud a spud,
No more lies or elaborate word contortions.
Chips are chips
Not pomme frites or french fries.
Why say 'haute cuisine' when you mean 'smaller portions'.

No more saying we had a 'tête à tête'
When you mean you've been nagging
Bragging or just chin wagging,

And no more calling it a 'menage à trois'
When you mean three people shagging.

I'm talking to someone else's father

I was, I suppose, gay around the age of 12 and 13.

Though to be honest, glandular activity being what it is, nothing was safe around that time. I'd have attempted sexual intercourse with a tin of swarfega if that was the only way of achieving orgasm.

It's important to declare this because there's thousands of men of all ages going round with the guilt of this development period shut away like a mutant twin, too ugly to be let into public gaze.

It is quite common for lads to become sexually aroused climbing over furniture. It is not considered incitement later in life to offer these people a chair when they visit.

The party to which you were not invited

'...was like no other party before.
What a party.
What a party.
Everyone was there.
Well, everyone, that is, but you.
It was incredible.
Amazing.
You wouldn't believe what went on.
I mean let's face it if you weren't at that party
then you don't know what PARTY means.
What a party.
You just couldn't imagine a party like that.
There'll never be a party like it again.
Everyone's still talking about it.
Well, everyone, that is, but you.
A party like that can change your life.
I mean any other party
is going to seem drab now in comparison.
I mean, I've been to parties with a capital P
but this was a party with a capital PARTY
know what I mean?
No, I don't suppose you do.
What a party.
A party like that comes once in a lifetime, maybe.
Still at least everyone can share the memory
well, everyone, that is,...'

There's always room in the hearse on the way back

Joseph plays the percentages.
He can be eyeing up four women in different parts of
the same room.
He takes his data day diary literally.
A wall chart of his sperm level would read like a cardiac arrest.
To him Love is a dog with six legs.
Relationships, just things that crash in the night.
Loyalty, a free fall from infatuation to indifference.
From the erotic to the erratic.

There is a need to prove that he can still compete.

To Joseph
Nature gives no time to niceties.
Forever, comes with in-built obsolescence.
There always appears a point in coupling when he feels like
he's stuck next to someone on a long coach journey having run
out of conversation.

In despair, it is of course the things we don't say that shout
the loudest.
Joseph mutilates his every hour.
I don't believe he chooses to be ugly
it is merely an ailment
a sickness of the spirit.

Joseph's crime is that of cowardice.
He has spent his whole life running with the eye of the storm
and destiny seems such a big word for such a small return.

Cranking up suspense in adolescence
     the pivot and swerve
     the running of the escalator
     carnal desire his internationale
Joseph shies away from the need of a meaning

For the ultimate taboo is to be lonely.
   even for a second
   and so to fail
   to be an object of pity
   to be a loser
and clichés become clichés for a reason
no one, but no one, loves a loser.

It is to strands of this
he ties his final submission.
   Hoping as mortality yawns.
   Hoping as the sediment thaws.
   Hoping as the essence pulls immediate to his breath
that his lies
are lies
after all.

All kids are born with long thin moustaches

Like most kids I suppose I was a natural surrealist.

I used to think nothing of playing football for hours in my cowboy outfit. I had no concept of relative scale and no distinct understanding of the comparative relationship between any two objects.

My Action Man would regularly hitch lifts straddled across a two-inch Matchbox fire-engine.

Toilet rolls, shoeboxes, Elastoplast reels, coat hangers and Fairy Liquid bottles were all stock multi-faceted components to fit into any imaginary playworld.

But never, and I always felt this to be one of the major drawbacks to my creativity, the double-sided sticky tape Blue Peter and Magpie presenters somehow always assumed you'd have lying around. For years I pictured all middle-class kids having drawers full of the stuff.

Large cardboard boxes could change in seconds from racing cars to jet planes or speed boats by just a slight alteration in the accompanying engine noise.

Any sheet or table cloth became a tent which I'd just sit in for days and days and days.

One of my very favourite games was when the British Eighth Army desert patrol Airfix soldiers would fight off the alien spaceship which was always made out of Lego and manned by Fuzzy-Felt farm animals.

A gift

At 7 o'clock this morning
I bring you a mountain.
I tap gently on your window
and you wake half covered in sleep.

'What's that?' you ask
'It's a mountain' I grin,
'I've carried it all night
I couldn't sleep so I brought it
here to show you.'
'What do I want with a mountain in my garden at 7 o'clock in
the morning?' you ask, not used to being woken at 7 o'clock with
a mountain in your garden.

I try to joke, now feeling a little embarrassed,
'It's for you, a gift.'
You say you don't want a mountain.
You are too tired to understand,
and I struggle to explain it's not the mountain I've brought you
it's the fact that I could bring it to you.
I strain to pick it up again and wonder what I'm going to do
    with it now.
I feel such a fool walking home with a mountain.

Tinned fruit and evaporated milk

So it was last Saturday tea time when I called in at my dad's. He was sat checking his racing results. I ambled across the room and turned off the TV. 'Just a second' I said tentatively before he started to protest, 'I've got something important to tell you'.

I hesitated a moment, then bracing myself I came right out with it, 'I love you dad' I said.

'Don't be so bloody daft,' he said.

'It's not daft', I said 'I love you.'

'Err...all right put kettle on then,' he said.

'No, you're supposed to say – I love you too son – c'mon dad you've seen *Dallas*.'

'I've not got time for all this bloody nonsense, I'm off to the Legion,' he said.

So I'm following him down the garden and I'm saying, 'Look dad I'm 34 now and I think it's about time it was out in the open, I love you.'

And he's trying to shh me in case the neighbours hear.

So I shout louder, 'I don't care if the whole world hears, I'm not ashamed of my feelings, I love you, you're my dad.' And I give him a big wet kiss on the forehead. 'What do you say dad, what do you say?'

'Oh Henry,' he said, 'Where did I go wrong?'

How the young and fashionable are feeling this season

They're wearing their
consciences well hid
this season. Hearts on
the sleeve are definitely
out. Compassion's out.
Basically the effect is not
to distract attention
from the expensive clothes.

Flunking the practical

It's easy to see now I must have upset the spontaneity of the occasion a little, leaping from bed after three and a half minute's extensive foreplay and rushing to the toilet there to wrestle with a Durex for the better part of an hour, but being inexperienced and easily embarrassed and knowing no better at the time it all seemed perfectly justified.

Once alone in the toilet I fumbled frantically in an effort to don my little passion accessory, my sexual fervour now waning fast due in no small measure to the cold toilet seat, the fact that it was her parents' toilet, the less than romantic atmosphere of the white woodchip walls and do-it-yourself plumbing, the ever lengthening gap in our mutual arousal and having tried unsuccessfully to roll the strange accoutrement on the wrong way twice, further blunting my ardour and leaving me with a task not dissimilar to stacking custard or trying to thread jelly into a pair of Doc Martens.

When eventually I slipped surreptitiously back under the blankets my sexual initiation recommenced cautiously. Although I'd taken a keen interest in the theory aspect at school there were still one or two points they were never too specific about in sex education classes.

Not mentioning that the sperm doesn't just disappear but can run back down a girl's leg when she stands up was one. The most important omission as far as I was concerned however was not explaining exactly how long the coitus activity should generally take. For four hours we hammered away trying to make sure that the job was done right. I didn't want her to think that I wasn't adequately potent and she didn't want to let on that she'd had enough three and a half hours since. All the next day we walked around exhausted and bruised, tender and inflamed, recovering from what felt effectively like a four-hour Chinese burn on the genitals.

I marvelled at friends who boasted that they did it every night thinking they must have really suffered.

The trainspotter of love

She was sophistication personified
an angel with hazel eyes
unmoved by my yearning
to my passion burning
          her indifference would not yield
as the train stopped
my hopes dropped
          and she got off at Macclesfield

A kind of loving

She came home one day and he'd gone.
In his favourite chair he'd left a yoghurt.
Unaccustomed to change
she lived with the yoghurt for three years.
It never moved from the chair.
They slept apart.
She often wondered if there was someone else.
It never ate what she served up.
It ignored relatives.
She would often have to hoover round it.
Her sister in law told her she was barmy
to stick it out this long
but she knew that marriage was something you had to work at.
She went to marriage guidance on her own
until they said they could do nothing further
if the yoghurt didn't accompany her on
the next visit.
Eventually she packed her bags and left.
It was a hard decision.
You can't live with a yoghurt for three years
without it leaving its mark on your life.
She had some fond memories though
of those early days,
and kept a photo of the yoghurt amongst her letters.

The ladies' man

He poured the word darling like acid
It ate
Through
Nameless
Women
Faceless
As the acid
Scoured
The flesh
From the bone
Darling – it smarted, keen to the touch
Darling – it stung, as it seeped into the conversation
He poured the darling like acid
Saying 'Don't worry your pretty little head now
          Don't worry your pretty little head.'

Stripper goes too far

Squeezing her voluptuous breasts she pouted
the front row sat erect
the climax they never doubted
they'd all come to expect
(but now a little extra)
pulling back her smile, she pulled her top lip
and slipped it over her head
the skull exposed, sheer and vile
veins ran worming purple and red
down over her shoulder the skin peeled onto the floor
now no one tried to hold her, no one squealed for more
then she tore out both of her mammary glands
the Joe on the front row had so craved
and taking one in each hand
she rubbed them into his face
next the flesh of her bottom she plucked from her torso
and placed on the Joe's knees
hadn't he got what he wanted but more so
you'd have thought he'd be pleased
finally she ripped out her womb by the fallopian tubes
and forced it down his throat
he seemed to lose his taste for sex abuse
so at least it ended on a happy note

The Acme God Company

Hire purchase with a higher purpose
Paradise privatised like a three-ring circus
Heaven on high at down to Earth prices
Sell yourself right out of a crisis
Sell yourself something you already own
for the Father and the Son are just a family firm
and lo
       the word of the Lord on the big board is quoted
as the Holy Spirit is finally floated
it's a preference share for Armageddon
see how the Dow Jones closes at Psalm one hundred and eleven
and behold
       the soul is sold from the National Health
so the poor that can't pay can go straight to Hell

and the Lord looked down on his Cherubim
lain broken on the ground with ruptured wings
and he wept

Time passed unnoticed until she took the clock

Slumped on your chair like dead weight at an orgy
coughing like an S-reg Fiat
though you've lit up a thousand churches in prayer
you know
         she's not coming back

Overfat on time, you say 'age doesn't matter' then you lie about
       your own
if you live to be 100 you'd still be afraid of dying too young
Switching off the bedside lamp shadows crowd the void
but the patterns on the wallpaper don't scare you any more
it's the blank spaces now that threaten
Nothing, not even love, survives within a vacuum

Fast approaching your love-by-date
you count the days left unkissed
Age
   has become just another stick to beat yourself with
Where once your passion was an elevator between Heaven and Hell
Where once you believed love dripped from between her legs
There in the absence of children
sex grew tired on easy living, becoming a parasite on the back
       of routine and all the words you chose so carefully
blew like so much litter
Conversations became quieter
and as scarce as a spaghetti western
Laughter became a missing person
until you couldn't remember kissing her face when you last made love
and her lips became just hooks to hang your heart upon
and though you look for that face from the window of every train
the photo in your pocket is now starting to fade
and though you curse the new diary with each year that arrives
you never noticed the clock on the wall until it kissed you goodbye
you never noticed the clock on the wall until it kissed you goodbye

The reflection in the back of God's spoon

Nude modelling for the afterlife
she secures the burger concession in Paradise

It's difficult to be concerned at the world's wrongs
with an industrial base of cream scones

There are dead moths at your altar
Theme parks replacing the landscapes of human nature

There's an empty funhouse with a formica carousel
A gardener nurturing humanity on the high road to Hell

Originality for the mass market reaped with a vengeance
individually wrapped tears and brutal indifference

As reproach stalks this poetry in thin disguise
for dogs bound by pavement there is little pride

All the seas of Mercy yet to understand
I feel the sadness of computers in an enchanted land

How can the Mortician fill dead bodies with formaldehyde
then go home and make love to his wife?

The wasting of limbs and the squandering of belief
Perpetual emotion and the dignity of trees
It's fear of death
beating the wings of my heart
I reach for your hand in the dark
I reach for your hand in the dark

Ten ways to end a relationship
(after Adrian Mitchell)

1. PATRIOTIC

I've got to dedicate myself to work of national importance.

2. SNOBBISH

Your time allocation has expired.

3. OVERWEENING

You are too fine a human to be held back by constraints.

4. PIOUS

I shall pray you find happiness elsewhere.

5. MELODRAMATIC

I'll kill myself rather than go through this torture any longer.

6. PATHETIC

I'm not worthy of love. I can't stand anyone to see me like this.

7. DEFENSIVE

I don't have to give any reasons.

8. SINISTER

I've been sleepwalking with a bread-knife lately.

9. LECHEROUS

I want to fuck your best friend.

10. PHILOSOPHICAL

Well were we really going out anyway?

Ostrich man

I can see no evil in the world
There's nothing can make me sad
I can't see anything because
My head's inside this bag

I'm not an animal, I'm a man
I was given this by my dad
He said one day everything you see will be yours
Then he gave me this bloody bag

The teachers gave me another
I got a further one from my mother
They gave me one at every job I had
They said 'we can see a great future for you son
          here wear this very nice bag'

But now I'm dead they say I can take it off
But though they think I'm mad
I'll show them they can't discipline me
See, I'm still wearing my bag

I showed them didn't I? I showed them

Only Christmas and birthdays bring death this close

Overnight
you have grown old
and though spite is no spur to succeed
in the absence of caress it can suffice

Only yesterday with hair dye and vitamins
you boasted you had cheated time
but now
it is the last dance of the party and
the prospect of a taxi home alone
rises like a flush within your cheeks

Years you wasted slip through the
doorway giggling together adolescent
Clear skin and eyes so bright
and always with partners that look such fools, but young
It is not them you hate but their youth
There is no individuality in this attraction merely the
aesthetics of innocence

and you, clinging to that one chance
force yourself into the night air before
the indignity of being the last to leave

I have seen you in the morning
lost in some mundane task
unaware of my presence
There is a subtlety of emotion that wisps around your eyes
You hesitate behind each door
    What worries you most is the loss of appetite
Where once you were so sure,
    diplomatic farewells have beaten back your pride
Where once you were curious,
    the nakedness of longing has sought to scar your faith
breathe still
breathe still
no whim of nature will chill your soul tonight

there are traditions that carry the truth of seasons
there are books that will outlast technology
we are old friends you and I
rest your fears against these words
it'll be all right
it will be all right.

Mime doesn't pay

Last night I was burgled by a mime artist. He never made a sound. He could have got away with it, but then he tried to steal a piano I haven't got.

He pushed and he pulled, he strained and he heaved, but it wouldn't move. Maybe he thought there was something valuable behind it. There wasn't. He tried to float the piano. He blew up a balloon and tied it to the piano, then he couldn't lift the balloon.

I found him in the morning trapped inside an imaginary box. I called the police. He started to panic. He tried climbing up a fictitious ladder. When the police arrived they let him out. He made a dash for it...tried running away on the spot.

It took the police four hours to get him into the car, he kept getting pulled back by an invisible rope. I decided not to press charges. This afternoon, I put in an insurance claim for the piano.

Undressing for sex when you feel you're getting fat

It's easy to tell if someone's self-conscious about being overweight
because when they undress for sex
they always take their trousers off
before their shirt.

Another dead giveaway
is the futile atttempt to hold their stomach in
whilst trying to pull off their socks.

With practise what usually happens is this –
firstly they make a bee-line for the side of the bed away from
the bedside lamp. Then back turned to both
the light and their partner
they slip down their trousers past their knees
whilst at the same time lowering themselves into the upright sitting
position on the edge of the bed.
Next, they step out of the trouser legs, tread off their socks, undo all
their shirt buttons, breath in and try in one swift movement
to discard their shirt and slip gracefully under the cover.

A complete waste of effort.
No one, but no one has a hope in Hell of ever enjoying sex
whilst trying to hold their breath.

Nevertheless, in the cold light of morning
they attempt once more to continue the deception and try desperately
to ooze out of bed unnoticed.

Confessions of a closet celibate

Now lust can rust 'cos I'm bored of sex
My libido's just a place where dust collects

You know the first signs of tedium are on their way
When you actually start snoring during foreplay

Then you can bemoan your hormones as really down the pan
When each orgasm seems like a predictable rhyme that takes too
Long to attain, and doesn't quite scan

Once a drug upon which I thrived

Now the insertion of protuding bits of the anatomy into the
Anatomy of another to effect a momentary sensation of pleasure
Together with a short period of well-being all seems somewhat
Too contrived

Where once during sex
To prolong the climax
I would go through the names of all the teams in the first
Division and mentally record them

Now I do the same with the second and third
Purely to prevent boredom

The mutually assured destruction of Mr and Mrs Jones

Like most arguments neither can remember who fired the first shot.
Both still had snipers positioned from their previous confrontations.
Both had started to build entrenchments. This time though it had
escalated into open conflict on a scale never seen before.
Mr Jones was flexing his muscles.
Mr Jones was about to demonstrate who wore the trousers.
Mrs Jones was beating the shit out of him.
In the aftermath there followed a period of chilled silence.
This Mr and Mrs Jones referred to as the cold war.
They built a wall between them. At first friends dropped in supplies.
Each began developing new weapons to inflict pain upon the other.
Each labelled their weapons 'deterrents'.
Each was determined if need be to 'deterrent' the other into oblivion.
Then gradually as paranoia became a firm enough basis to build upon
peace talks began.
But if one day either of their tongues should slip...

Victims of war

Victims of War building week by week into a sickening reminder of the inhuman slaughter conveniently overlooked by glossy colour magazines for war enthusiasts.

At last after 40 years of sweeping the shame under the carpet *Victims of War* brings you full page photographs of sinews and bones blown from a child's naked corpse.

Marvel at authentic maps of mass murder illustrated in colour with diagrams depicting the distasteful side of war, the deformity of war veterans, the deaths through disease and decay, the mutilated bodies caught strewn across bomb-sites before being laid neatly in rows, grassed over and decorated with clean white headstones that never show the blood.

Follow train load by train load the hell of the holocaust in all its ugly fascination.

Collect the close-up pictures of concentration camps not quite cleansed of the stench of death before the first train load of American tourists.

Read personal eye-witness accounts of the pain and the grief, recapture the pitiful degrading of humanity. *Victims of War* available at little cost. Buy World War One, get World War Two free.

The human meat

Rubbing the monkey into her face
She felt more attractive already
The heart of a rabbit she used
To highlight her cheekbones
Assorted rodents she smoothed to her lips
Woodlice, cockroaches and other insects
Darkened her lashes
Whilst the blinded eyes of labradors
She dabbed behind her ears
For the final touch
She slipped into a full length mink
Turning to leave she
Caught sight of her
Reflection and squealed
With excitement
Tonight she was dressed to kill

You never see a bright yellow hearse

The English don't die they just become discreet
You never see a hearse clamped on Harley Street
Or parked at a picnic sight
Near Lovers' Leap

You never see a hearse outside a betting shop
Left next to a row of prams
You never see the route to the cemetery
Served by special hearse trams

You never see a hearse at a wedding
Or on adverts for banks
Or a row of hearses at a military parade
Behind a squadron of tanks

Or outside a nightclub at closing time
With racing stripes down the bonnet
Or a hearse at the Motor Show
With dead models draped upon it

You never see a double decker hearse
Or a hearse that's extra wide
Or a hearse with four or five coffins
All crammed up inside

You never see a coffin in a side car
For a fanatical ex-biker
Or a hearse at a transport café
Picking up a hitch-hiker

You never see a hearse used for ram-raiding
Or a hearse with fluffy dice
Or a hearse with a taxi meter
So you can keep an eye on the price

You never see a hearse at an auction
Some dealer's trying to flog
Or a hearse with a trailer
For someone who died with their dog

Each hearse is black and clean and neat
Because the English don't die they just become discreet

Southern Cemetery – The class of '92

Like comic timing
Old graves
Bedded well in hard ground
Sit easy in glib abstract

With assurance of place
Haircuts grown out
Mourners long since rejoined
Our great grandfathers surrender their individuality

   In the grandeur of their anonymity
   We grieve more for humanity than our own mortality

Then we come upon God's latest crop
Fresh mounds of loose soil
Soft like a hand on your brow
A scar still pink before the skin hardens

There's something disturbing
About the grouping of these
Well tended plots at the edge of gate

The unweathered granite
The unworn epitaphs
Like first year kids in their new uniforms
As rich and as brown as a new satchel

Anxious like their mother
We hesitate at the railings
'Take care of her Uncle John'
'Take care of her'

On the far side of the high street
There's a choice of undertakers
And a discreet distance down the road you can buy flowers

The couple nextdoor – A sharing experience

The couple in the flat next door are always considerate enough to save their arguments until it's time for bed.

This selfless gesture ensures that their intimate secrets, their sexual inadequacies, inferiority and persecution complexes, petty jealousies, childhood traumas, parental rejections, adolescent failings, perverse lust fantasies, unfulfilled animal needs, and their constant insecurity in the other's commitment to the relationship are all that much easier for us to enjoy.

The annoying thing is though that he insists on whimpering in a weak pathetic whine that's very difficult to make out. She on the other hand has perfect diction through a wide range of levels from full pitch screaming right up to violent hysterical frenzy, at which she is particularly entertaining. It seems a general rule for both that the logic content of the argument decreases in direct proportion to the volume and speed of delivery. Another annoying habit he has is that of speaking away from the adjoining wall and I get a feeling sometimes that he's a little embarrassed at what he's actually saying. She however grasps every opportunity to exploit this weakness and gain the upper hand by repeating his sentences word for word in the form of a very loud exclamation mark.

A problem they share jointly is the frequent compulsion to storm off into another room after a particularly good line. Other distractions include the unnecessarily long pauses often mistaken for premature aborting of the conflict leaving both participants and spectators alike with a frustrating sense of anti-climax, and the sporadic fits of door banging that can so often surprise even the most careful of listeners causing any glass not firmly held to make that embarrassing smashing sound as it drops from your ear to the foot of the wall. Possibly the most pitifully pathetic and therefore most interesting phase of the argument usually comes when he's ready to make up but she's not quite ready. For the next six or seven minutes he's apologetic and condescending, then after one too many rejections he suddenly blows his top stomping around and shouting such memorable classics as 'I'm trying to be nice to you, you stupid prat!' I don't think he's actually ever hit her though she's been violent, often unnervingly violent many times, but once I understand in desperation trying to disperse the anger he spat full in her face. You could tell from the immediate reaction that he knew even as it happened it was the worst thing he could do. Listening to two broken people crying in the night can suddenly make you feel very lonely. At this point I usually hug my girlfriend tight and thank God that tonight the argument was next door.

A farce is still a farce even with subtitles

and she tells me she loves him
with her hand stroking my inner thigh
Her face is symmetrical and her sweat has a pleasant composition
We are exchanging pretty lies like cigarette cards
Stifling disinterest like two old soldiers between battles
The mutual gratification of animal lust seems a distinct possibility
We are both whores to romance
but it is all too predictable
There is no pilgrimage in her finger-tips
only the musing of calculation
and I wonder if my face displays its weariness
Bone clumsy
an idle stubble scratches the sheen from her make-up
There is no nourishment in these overtures
only the mechanics of anatomy, a series of shrugs
How can your blood race so fast
but your heart remain unmoved
I don't have to wait for the morning to hate myself
Pitiful and pathetic seem insults too well used to scald disgust
When I look into the mirror, if I concentrate on the centre
features of my face, I can see how I used to look in my teens
Is it guilt that's swollen my neck
or my face wrapping itself against the world?
The desire to wipe the slate clean, to start a new jotter,
competes each day against the easier option to drown all vivid
images in maudlin and lay, before God's feet, face down in the
subway, stained with my own piss
As you can see I try my best to romanticise this predicament
but tacky affairs always remind of cheap early seventies movies.

Breaking up is...

Breaking up is...
making a conscious effort to say 'I' instead of 'we'
taking your number down from beside the phone
trying to play only records you never liked
pretending to be busy
trying to think of people worse off
mutual friends being diplomatic, saying 'at least you're both
      still young'
and 'at least you've got your health'
and other sentences all starting with 'at least'
planning the weekend around half a dozen eggs
not knowing what to do with hands when walking down the street
finding people who look like you attractive
forgiving you everything then nothing every other minute
discounting years in seconds
wanting to talk but wishing too much hadn't been said already

The breath within the balloon

The breath within the balloon
will not last.
You never get inflated balloons
on the *Antiques Roadshow*.
Breath brings with it vulnerability.

If never inflated
a balloon may last forever
but such limp reason
will never enchant a child
                        with decoration
or gladden the heart
with the stretching of possibility
and the fulfilment of promise.

Is not a universe of such balloons sadder
than a universe where balloons are apt to burst.

I hold your breath within my hands.

The breath within the balloon will not last
but the giving of breath
and the tying of the knot
at each new birth
is an offering
for our choice of worlds.

Flux could kill

The grass leans outward
The cliff
jagged with purpose
penetrates the waves

Two feet from certain death
Two feet of existence
not menacing but matter of fact
The choice is always as narrow as this
Only here
you can measure spirit

Two feet of lies and soft options
Two feet of fear and pulse
There is a truth that's too easy to forget until you fill your
lungs with determination

At times such as dusk
there is wonder in the commonplace

Rain hangs on the skyline

Beauty is always this short a distance

I have spent my whole life trying to enter the gates of Heaven
using my heart as a battering ram

Two feet of the attainable
Two feet from acceptance

Travelling second class through Hope

With softer spine you rise and shine
And strap yourself safe in time
More beads for the natives, more gongs for the troops,
You buy off the kids with spaghetti hoops
Melt into the monotone, the drip-feed TV
Death Wish 4, *Funland UK*, until you say
Is   this   all   there   is?

You say you need a cause, you need to fight
You're looking for something, anything
If only you had something noble denied
You say sometimes you'd fight everything
So down at the beast market
You seek solace in your crisps
Hey what's a nice Jaeger jumper like that
Doing in a place like this?
You see Madonna singing *Material Girl*
To earthquake victims in the Third World
You see a white car drive through Soweto
Swords designed as shields
The new credit card diplomacy
And the worship of God on wheels, and you say
Is   this   all   there   is?

And when the party's over, and limp lettuce and lager trodden
into the carpet are no longer part of the fun. And you realise
that the Earth doesn't revolve around three pubs in the centre
of town. And you realise your God's not bigger than my God
after all. Travelling second class through Hope, you pray, there
must be more than this.

The night my heart caught fire

The blue lights flashed like a cheap disco at a wedding
six firemen in yellow hats and matching trousers
jumped out of the red engine and the hoses pissed forth.
As damp rapidly became an understatement
                    a white hat took charge.
'That's the worst case of heartburn I've ever seen' he joked
dragging me unconscious from the wreckage. When eventually
        I came to I
checked my inside pockets – I was in luck, they'd not wet my matches.